THE IN WORD

THE IN WORD

The 2 letters that will change your life

CYNTHIA ROBINSON

La Verne Spruill

Cynthia Robinson LLC

Contents

Acknowledgment

First, I am giving honor to my Heavenly Father, who is the head of my life. To Jesus, my Savoir and groom. To the Holy Spirit, that is my constant friend.

To my family, thank you all for your support as I become a better daughter, mother and wife.

To Laverne Spruill for always being a great editor for me.

To all my brothers and sisters in Christ, let's get ready to talk.

I

No Blood Required by Author Cynthia Robinson

18 When I say unto the wicked, Thou shalt surely die; and thou givest him not warning, nor speakest to warn the wicked from his wicked way, to save his life; the same wicked man shall die in his iniquity; but his blood will I require at thine hand.

19 Yet if thou warn the wicked, and he turn not from his wickedness, nor from his wicked way, he shall die in his iniquity; but thou hast delivered thy soul.

20 Again, when a righteous man doth turn from his righteousness, and commit iniquity, and I lay a stumbling-block before him, he shall die: because thou hast not given him warning, he shall die in his sin, and his righteousness which

he hath done shall not be remembered; but his blood will I require at thine hand.

21 Nevertheless if thou warn the righteous man, that the righteous sin not, and he doth not sin, he shall surely live, because he is warned; also thou hast delivered thy soul. Ezekiel 3:18-21

It goes without saying that I love my God and I am thankful for what He has, will, and is, doing within me.

I am truly in love with all He is doing in me and for the work ahead. It may seem hard at times, but it is needful for the harvest that He has given to me to bear fruit. I do not take on this task lightly, but I do take it on and will work it with His help.

2

Preface for "IN"

The "IN" word is a simple yet complex book on being "IN" a relationship with God. We cannot just be Christian or religious people. At the point of adoption into the family of God, everything in our lives changes. We are no longer on the outside looking in. No more just being Gentiles or Jews. Not sinners doomed to hell for eternity. The confession of your mouth that Jesus Christ came to die for your sins and that His resurrection confirmed eternal life with the Godhead, we are now heirs with Christ.

With that being said, to be "IN" means we have something we must do. We are to be "IN" relationship with God. Now, I know some of you are saying, "I'm already in a relationship with God. I pray daily, I read my Bible, and I go to church. I sing in the choir, I minister to the young/the elderly, and I do other ministry work. I give to the poor, and I do missions work out of the country. I pay tithes and offerings." "My relationship with God is fine. Is it, really?" Everything mentioned are *works* for the Kingdom. It's good, but what about the "IN" God part? Merriam-Webster defines the word "IN" as *used in a function to indicate inclusion, location, or position within limits.*

After reading this definition, what type of relationship do you have with the Godhead? Are you "Having" a relationship or "With" God "IN" a relationship, or are you "In" a relationship with God? Let's see...

The relationship with God is like the Tabernacle in the Old Testament. It is divided into 3 parts the outer court, the inner court and The Holy of Holies. Each is a place where the Lord will meet you. Once you begin to move forward in your relationship, changes will take place, and the bond becomes stronger.

One of the Pastors I had the pleasure of serving with in ministry taught this subject very well. He stated, "We, being the tabernacle, are divided into percentages, 30%, 60%, and 90%. No one is 100%. That happens in heaven. I always liked that. I desired to be at 90%. I did not know what 90% looked like. Did it look like going to church every day and reading the Bible several times a day? Did it happen when you are married to a man/woman you loved like Jesus loved the church? Is it when you are working for the church in ministry and giving your all to the people?

That all sounds good, but that is not it. When God

instructed them on the building of the Tabernacle, the Holy of Holies was for 1 person. Only Priests who were cleansed with a pure heart and reverenced God were allowed to enter and communion with Him. Wait. You mean I have to go to God alone?

I can't bring my mother, grandmother or Pastor with me? I thought that church membership was enough? I mean, I pay my tithes and always give in the freewill offering. Now you're talking about being in a relationship with God that requires just the 2 of us? The answer is a 3 letter word, YES.

We have to grow within the Godhead. We have to clean out our tabernacles and work to be in a relationship with God. This does not come easily. We have to work on our Faith 30%, Truth 60%, and Love 90% of God.

I know some of you are saying, "Faith should be 90%, and maybe you are right, but in order to hear God, we have to have faith that He is speaking to us.

Jesus says that if we have faith the size of a mustard seed, we can move mountains. Faith is the first step, then trust and last but not least, love.

3

"HAVE"

To hold or maintain as a possession, privilege, or entitlement.

To have a relationship with the Godhead has a good and bad side to it. First, we all should have a relationship with God. This relationship starts at the moment of salvation. When we give our lives over to the Lord, we surrender our will for God's will. The Godhead will affect and effect both our personal and spiritual lives. We will begin to see things differently because God's word becomes life to us. We begin to want what God has for us and desire the faith to believe in Him completely.

We start receiving the blessings and promises of God. God begins to pour out privileges that were once ours before the fall of man. We get to be with Him as Adam and Eve were having an intimate relationship with God. No barriers, no boundaries, just us, Spirit filled beings.

Sidebar: We MUST worship God in spirit and in truth in order to be "IN" relationship. Flesh can't be there. When we cry out, He is there to answer our call. Like a good Father, He shows up.

I remember when I started having a relationship with God. It seemed so easy to get a prayer through. I could just call Him, and whatever I was in need of, it came to me. I can't count the times when food was brought to me, money put in my hand, or an unexpected check came in the mail. The privilege of being a child of God was amazing. God will hold fast to his word.

The Bible tells us from Genesis to Revelation that God is

present in our lives. There are 525 combinations of the word God and references to His relationship with us. I am going to list a few here.

God gave us dominion

"And God said, Let us make man in our image, after our likeness: and let them have dominion over the fish of the sea, and over the fowl of the air, and over the cattle, and over all the earth, and over every creeping thing that creepeth upon the earth." Genesis 1:26

God will preserve what is His

"And Jacob called the name of the place Peniel: for I have seen God face to face, and my life is preserved." Genesis 32:30

God has given His Spirit

"And I have filled him with the spirit of God, in wisdom, and in understanding, and in knowledge, and in all manner of workmanship." Exodus 31:3

Have not God commanded

"Have not I commanded thee? Be strong and of a good courage; be not afraid, neither be thou dismayed: for the Lord thy God is with thee whithersoever thou goest." Joshua1:9

God has mercy on me

"Hear me when I call, O God of my righteousness: thou hast enlarged me when I was in distress; have mercy upon me, and hear my prayer." Psalm 4:1

I have put my trust
"In God have I put my trust: I will not be afraid what man can do unto me." Psalm 56:11

Have Faith
"And Jesus answering saith unto them, Have faith in God." Mark 11:22

We have a great high priest
"Seeing then that we have a great high priest, that is passed into the heavens, Jesus the Son of God, let us hold fast our profession." Hebrew 4:14

We have been sealed
"Saying, Hurt not the earth, neither the sea, nor the trees, till we have sealed the servants of our God in their foreheads." Revelation 7:3

These verses are just a few examples of how important having a relationship with God is and what it looks like. This is the positive side.

What happens when you have a relationship with God?

4

Having a Relationship
with God

The change happens when we start taking for granted the blessings and promises of God. We stop seeing God's mercy towards us and started believing that we are His children and He should just give us everything and everything we want. This can easily happen when our motives are in the wrong place.

One of the ways this happened within the church was the prosperity movement in the late 70s. This movement believed in Abraham's blessings which is our rightful inheritance. The problem is this. When we go to God with an attitude of entitlement, we are in the wrong. When your thoughts are," I'm supposed to..." and not "I am grateful for," you change the relationship you have with God. You have flipped it. Instead of receiving God's privileges, you have turned it into a "my entitlement." Your attitude is, "God better give it to me." Don't believe me? I have an example.

One of the best examples of entitlement is the Prodigal Son parable in the book of Luke 15:11-32.

12 And the younger of them said to his father, Father, give me the portion of goods that falleth to me. And he divided unto them his living.

13 And not many days after the younger son gathered all together, and took his journey into a far country, and there wasted his substance with riotous living.

14 And when he had spent all, there arose a mighty famine in that land; and he began to be in want.

15 And he went and joined himself to a citizen of that country; and he sent him into his fields to feed swine.

16 And he would fain have filled his belly with the husks that the swine did eat: and no man gave unto him.

17 And when he came to himself, he said, How many hired servants of my father have bread enough and to spare, and I perish with hunger!

18 I will arise and go to my father, and will say unto him, Father, I have sinned against heaven, and before thee,

19 And am no more worthy to be called thy son: make me as one of thy hired servants.

20 And he arose, and came to his father. But when he was yet a great way off, his father saw him, and had compassion, and ran, and fell on his neck, and kissed him.

21 And the son said unto him, Father, I have sinned against heaven, and in thy sight, and am no more worthy to be called thy son.

²² But the father said to his servants, Bring forth the best robe, and put it on him; and put a ring on his hand, and shoes on his feet:

²³ And bring hither the fatted calf, and kill it; and let us eat, and be merry:

²⁴ For this my son was dead, and is alive again; he was lost, and is found. And they began to be merry.

²⁵ Now his elder son was in the field: and as he came and drew nigh to the house, he heard music and dancing.

²⁶ And he called one of the servants, and asked what these things meant.

²⁷ And he said unto him, Thy brother is come; and thy father hath killed the fatted calf, because he hath received him safe and sound.

²⁸ And he was angry, and would not go in: therefore came his father out, and entreated him.

²⁹ And he answering said to his father, Lo, these many years do I serve thee, neither transgressed I at any time thy commandment: and yet thou never gavest me a kid, that I might make merry with my friends:

³⁰ But as soon as this thy son was come, which hath devoured thy living with harlots, thou hast killed for him the fatted calf.

³¹ And he said unto him, Son, thou art ever with me, and all that I have is thine.

³² It was meet that we should make merry, and be glad: for this thy brother was dead, and is alive again; and was lost, and is found.

I hope you took a moment to read it. If you did, was there a verse that stuck out to you? Verse 12 should be ringing in your mind. It says,

"And the younger of them said to his father, Father, give me the portion of goods that falleth to me. And he divided unto them his living."

Give me is what he said was his. How many of us approach God the Father, God the Son, and God the Holy Spirit/Ghost with a "give me" attitude. We come with scriptures in our mouths but deception in our hearts. We want what we want, when we want it, how we want it, and at the time we want it. We have turned God into a genie and placed him in a bottle. We come along, rubbing the bottle (praying) when we need God (the genie) to help us out. When the wishes (blessings or promises) are not answered the way we want them to be, we blame everybody and God.

This is the 30%'ers. These people have faith, but it is not in God for who He is but for what He will give them. They are **the outer court** people. They may burn off some of the flesh, but not all. They don't trust Him or love Him. Like the prodigal son, they look at what their Father has as theirs because they are heirs. What they do not realize is that a true heir does not just receive but also has to give. We have to give God our unbelief so our faith can mature and be sustained through unanswered prayers. Our trust in Him has to be built up in order to get past what we see. Our love has to grow so we can love despite the hurt that comes because of flesh (ours and others).

Psalms 37:-3-5 gives us a roadmap on the way that we should live our lives in the presence of God.

> *3 Trust in the Lord, and do good; so shalt thou dwell in the land, and verily thou shalt be fed.*
> *4 Delight thyself also in the Lord: and he shall give thee the desires of thine heart.*
> *5 Commit thy way unto the Lord; trust also in him; and he shall bring it to pass.*

The roadmap is clear on what we need to do, how we need to do it, and why we need to do it.

1. Trust in the Lord-verse3
2. Do good-verse3
3. Delight thyself also in the Lord-verse4
4. Commit thy ways unto the Lord-verse5

When we do these steps, this will happen:

1. We will dwell in the land-verse3
2. We will be feed-verse3
3. He shall give us the desires of our heart-verse 4
4. He will bring it to pass-verse 5

When we do our part in developing our relationship with God and not just the blessings He gives, we can enjoy being heirs with Jesus Christ. We will be able to live in privilege and not entitlement. The reason we cannot live in entitlement is because we did not purchase God. He purchased us with the blood of His Son. *1 Peter 1:18-19.*

18 For you know that you were not redeemed from your useless [spiritually unproductive] way of life inherited [by tradition] from your forefathers with perishable things like silver and gold, 19but [you were actually purchased] with precious blood, like that of a [sacrificial] lamb unblemished and spotless, the priceless blood of Christ. AMP

Sidebar: Do not take the blood of Jesus for granted

The "Have" Questions

Do you have a good relationship with God?

Do you have a genie relationship with God?

Do you take for granted the blessings of God toward you?

Do you need to repent from a "Give Me" mindset?

Prayer of Repentance

Dear Father, I am so sorry. I have taken your blessings toward me as a given and not as a gift. I ask you to forgive me for my entitlement mindset, and I pray that from this moment on, I will walk with grace and mercy trusting in you for all things, in Jesus's name, Amen.

Notes

5

"With" God

With, used as a function word to indicate a participant
in an action, transaction, or arrangement

"With God" is not a bad position. When we are with God, we are participating with Him. We are talking, listening, and meditating with God, and that's not bad.

The words "with God" are combined 732 times in the Bible. This means that being "with" God is where we should be. I have pulled out several examples of being with God. These are only a few:

Enoch walked with God

"And Enoch walked with God: and he was not; for God took him." Genesis 5:24

God talked with Abram

"And Abram fell on his face: and God talked with him, saying ..." Genesis 17:3

God girds with strength

"It is God that girdeth me with strength, and maketh my way perfect." Psalm 18:32

God's song shall be with me

"Yet the Lord will command his lovingkindness in the day time, and in the night his song shall be with me, and my prayer unto the God of my life." Psalm 42:8

God is with us

"Take counsel together, and it shall come to nought; speak the word, and it shall not stand: for God is with us." Isaiah 8:10

God dealt wondrously with you

"And ye shall eat in plenty, and be satisfied, and praise the name of the Lord your God, that hath dealt wondrously with you: and my people shall never be ashamed. "Joel 2:26

The word is always with God

"In the beginning was the Word, and the Word was with God, and the Word was God. The same was in the beginning with God." John 1:1-2

You are with the household of God

"Now therefore ye are no more strangers and foreigners, but fellow citizens with the saints, and of the household of God;" Ephesians 2:19

As you can see, being with God is a life full of blessings. You get to know God as a Father, Jesus as a Savior and the Holy Spirit/Ghost as a Comforter. God the Father is no longer a cold and distant God but one that you can depend upon. You look forward to learning more about Him and how you are to be an active part of the kingdom of God.

You begin to arrange your life around everything that is God. You are reading the Bible daily, desiring the sincere milk of the word. You go to church every time the doors are open. You are in two different ministries in the church. You watch what comes into your life because you don't want anything coming in between you and your relationship with God. He is your everything!

I remember when I was "with God" that way. For 5 years, I only listened, watched and stayed around fellow Christians. If the Godhead was not a part of it, I didn't want anything to do with it. The problem with this is when someone or something comes to challenge you (my challenge was a man, and I fell away for 13 years to follow Islam), your relationship can quickly change.

6

With you and God

When you are challenged in your relationship with God, you will either accept the challenge or trust God that you don't have to participate in that conversation or behavior. You may be saying to yourself, "What challenge?" The challenge is coming against your faith and trust in God. We either believe that God will do what He said He would do, or we step in and make the decision for Him. When you decide that you can make decisions for God about your life, you will fall and fall quickly. Don't believe me? Maybe the stories (yes stories) of Sarai and Abram (the father of our blessings) will speak some truth to what I am saying.

God, Abram and Sarai have a history that started before they became Abraham and Sarah. It starts in **Genesis 12** when God called Abram from out among his family, country and people. Abram heard and obeyed God to a certain extent. Abram left as God instructed, but he took his nephew Lot with him. **(Genesis 12:5).**

Sometimes we participate with God but then switch the arrangement, around or slightly, to make ourselves comfortable.

A sidebar: You have to become comfortable with being uncomfortable. Growth lives there.

Back to the story. They leave, and their first challenge is with the prince of Egypt, that was attracted to Sarai. Abram asked her to say that she was his sister. Really!!! I mean, he isn't lying. She is his sister, but "they're married now." His fear of dying and not relying on the promises of God caused him to switch the arrangements. Doubt, fear and shame will make us change our relationship with God. You will no longer participate in the promises but reject your own blessings. Abram did this not just once but twice. He almost got 2 groups of people killed because of his feelings. Does that sound familiar - being "IN" your feelings?

Faith, trust and loving God will get you to see the spirit and not the flesh.

The next time they decided to change their participation with God was with the promise of the birth of their son, Isaac. God comes to Abram and says that he will have a man child (*Genesis 15: 4-5*). After waiting a little too long for God to give them their child, they decide that the arrangements God had were not what they wanted. They wanted a child now and decided to "help God" along.

In *Genesis 16:1-4. Now Sarai Abram's wife bare him no children: and she had a handmaid, an Egyptian, whose name was Hagar.*

²And Sarai said unto Abram, Behold now, the Lord hath restrained me from bearing: I pray thee, go in unto my maid; it may be that I may obtain children by her. And Abram hearkened to the voice of Sarai.

³And Sarai Abram's wife took Hagar her maid the Egyptian, after Abram had dwelt ten years in the land of Canaan, and gave her to her husband Abram to be his wife.

⁴And he went in unto Hagar, and she conceived: and when she saw that she had conceived, her mistress was despised in her eyes.

Messy, Messy, Messy! They stopped participating in a

relationship with God. They thought God was taking too long. God told Abram and Sarai that they would have a child, but the "when" was not answered.

Often, we want to know when, instead of just being grateful that we will receive a blessing as a result of the faithful promises of God. We want to go into council with God about all of the details. We start acting like we are on the same level as God. We forget that God is the Alpha and Omega, the beginning and the Ending *(Revelation 1:8)*. We forget that He is the Author and Finisher of our faith *(Hebrew12:2)*. He knows your life because He made us *(Jeremiah 1:5)*. Peter says it best in *2 Peter 3:8*, *"But, beloved, be not ignorant of this one thing, that one day is with the Lord as a thousand years, and a thousand years as one day.* This statement would mean that God knows our lives completely. There are no questions He has not answered. No problems He has not already solved. No trials or tribulations that we will encounter that He does not know the end results.

This is when we are in the 60%. We have faith and a little trust but no love. God is still not just a Father to us but God to us. He is our Savior, but we need to learn more about what Jesus Christ and His finished works accomplished for us. The Holy Spirit dwells on the inside of us, but He is either something we still fear or someone that makes us dance.

As we go into The Holy of Holies, we have work to do. We have to learn what the lighting of the golden candles means, where to place the showbread and when to burn the incenses.

This requires learning and mastering the priesthood. We are all called to the priesthood, and we must be able to go before God for ourselves. A verse in *1 Peter 2:5* says exactly that.

"Ye also, as lively stones, are built up a spiritual house, a holy priesthood, to offer up spiritual sacrifices, acceptable to God by Jesus Christ."

The priesthood is a God-ordained position. It is for His honor and for His glory. He places us in this role in order to continue the spiritual "sacrificing."

Knowing this, why do we give in to doubt, fear and shame and allow these things to cause us to walk in a different direction than God's promise?

God's Challenge

Back to the story, we know that Abraham and Sarah had a son, Isaac. *(Genesis 21:1-3)* but another challenge arises. God asks for a sacrifice *(Genesis 22)*. That sacrifice is not a bull, lamb or goat but his only promised son. God had given him the promise, and was He going to take it back? Abraham did not flinch. He prepared the sacrifice. He believed. He trusted. He loved. He knew that if God did it before, He could do it again.

Have you been here, where God has given you something that He promised, and it looks like it is going to be taken away, a job, man, woman, home or even a child? The signs are all there. It is about to slip through your fingers. We say to ourselves, "God said I could have it." "Why God, Why? "

The reason is because you trust Him as far as you can see the promise. When it looks like it is slipping through your fingers, you begin to go from 60 to 50 to 40 percent. Your faith and trust in God are wavering. God needs you solid as a rock. Not tossing back and forth. You are going to have trials and tribulations come into your life. You are going to have the impossible happen, and you must believe that if He did it before with you, He would do it again for you. The Lord is not slack concerning His promises. He will never make you suffer without a way of escape.

God never tempts us more than we can handle. *(1 Cor.10:13)* He knows the outcome way before the challenge presents itself. God knows your level of faith in Him, your trust in Him and your love for Him.

Abraham was ready, and you know, funny thing, so was Isaac. Isaac followed his Father to later be the sacrifice that God was asking for. He answered the challenge with thought of "God, thy will be done." Abraham learned what it meant to be "with" God. Abraham was not only with God at that moment. He was "IN" God. He was "IN" the Holy of Holies. Abraham trusted and believed in God.

God asked Abraham a question that we all need to ponder

when it comes to our own doubts and fears about the promises of God in our lives.

"Is anything too hard for the Lord? At the time appointed I will return unto thee, according to the time of life, and Sarah shall have a son." Genesis 18:14

"With" Questions

Are you "with" God? Yes or No

Are you a participant, or are you making the arrangements?

Are you holding up your blessings and promises from God because of doubt, fear or shame?

Repentance prayer

Dear Father, I am asking in the name of Jesus to please forgive me for doubting your love towards me. You have loved me from the beginning and will love me until the end. I place all my cares (doubts, fear and shame) in your hands, and I trust that from this day on, you have everything in complete order. Whatever you ask of me, I will do knowing that you have planned my life in your perfect design. In Jesus's name, Amen.

Notes:

7

"IN"

Used as a function word to indicate inclusion, location, or position within limits.

The "IN" word has two different meanings for me in this book. The first is on the previous pages from Merriam-Webster's Dictionary definition. The second one comes from me. If you have never read any of my other books, I am an acronyms and words play girl. I love changing words into acronyms. I believe that every word, no matter how small or big, can have several meanings. I know that God feels this way because God is the Word, and the Word has been since the conception of the world. *(Genesis 1:1 John1:3)*

This chapter talks about the "IN" word and its meaning from my viewpoint, and then I will go into the "IN" word meaning toward the subject of the Godhead. Each one of them has a word that corresponds to the definition of "IN." They are the following:

- God the Father- Inclusion
- God the Son- Position
- God the Holy Ghost Spirit- Location

Each one has a separate "IN" to our lives. If we exclude any part, we miss the Triune God and the opportunity to become Kingdom dwellers. We will stay in a constant fight with ourselves for the liberty God freely offers to us. We will also either stay, having a relationship "IN" God or just being "with" God. We cannot stay there. We have to go deeper. Aaron did not stay on the outside. He went into the Holy of Holies. My brothers and sisters, so should we. When we go into the Holy of Holies, we are at 90%.

Now I am going to tell what the "IN" word means from my viewpoint. The word means "Impossible Necessity." We must come to the realization that we have to live daily in the impossible with God, and that is a necessity.

I say this because our relationship "IN" God is based on the impossible. The definition of impossible means *incapable of being or of occurring: felt to be incapable of being done, attained, or fulfilled: insuperably difficult.*

Do you see it? You have to believe that what is incapable of being can exist. That thing that cannot be done, attained or fulfilled will be done, attained and fulfilled. What does that sound like to you? How does that feel? When should you see it? Isn't the impossible possible with God? Absolutely!

Wait! Before we get ahead of ourselves, we have to define another word, necessity. Necessity is defined as *the quality or state of being necessary.* The word is a noun. That means it includes all people, places and things. We must know that no matter the situation or circumstance or people, God has already made the provision for it to work out. This can only work if we have these three things in motion: faith, love and trust. There is no way we can be "IN" God if we do not have faith in Him and what he will do for his people. His love was there way before we knew who HE was and who He would be in our lives. Trusting in Him and His ability is a must! We can't be saved, transformed or develop if these are not our primary agendas.

Now, I know some of you are saying, "I have faith in God!" Do you REALLY??? I thought I did, too, until God helped me to realize I didn't have Kingdom-minded faith. Kingdom and earthly faith are different. Earthly faith is having or "with" God by faith. This faith is moved by our feelings and lust. If you don't remember, please go back and read the chapters on "Have" and "With." That faith works when you have everything you want, and you don't feel pressure to change into an heir of God. You are contented with the same people in your life, the same places and things around you that don't stretch you but allow you to stay stagnant and stale. You don't read your Bible or pray daily. It's only when you are in trouble that you apply these necessary habits. This is a "genie" relationship or a Child/God relationship. You put all of your issues and concerns before God, but you don't believe Him to "really" fix things for you. You put your hands on everything instead of having faith that with God, all things are possible. Then, when your issues and concerns turn into trials, tribulations and headaches, you blame God because he didn't answer your prayers in your time frame or the way you felt He should have answered.

Kingdom faith is built on the following scriptures:

Jesus said:
"And Jesus said unto them, Because of your unbelief: for verily I say unto you, If ye have faith as a grain of mustard seed, ye shall say unto this mountain, Remove hence to yonder place;

and it shall remove; and nothing shall be impossible unto you."
Matthew 17:20

Have faith in Who?

"And Jesus answering saith unto them, Have faith in God."
Mark 11:22

Touch me

"Then saith He to Thomas, Reach hither thy finger, and behold my hands; and reach hither thy hand, and thrust it into my side: and be not faithless, but believing." John 20:27

What is your profession?

"Let us hold fast the profession of our faith without wavering; (for he is faithful that promised;)" Hebrews 11:39

The faith scripture for life

"Now faith is the substance of things hoped for, the evidence of things not seen." Hebrews 11:1

When your faith relies solely on substance (things), you do not have faith in God; you have doubt. You believe in the things and not the One who created the things. Your faith is easily moved because when the "things" do not appear or go away, so does your relationship with God.

Kingdom faith is the foundation that will hold you in place no matter the storm, no matter the trial, no matter the situation. You will believe God because He said it, and He will make it so. No, you don't have it, nor is it with you, but God is "IN" you, and so is His word.

I'm going to leave you with this scripture. ***"But seek ye first the kingdom of God, and his righteousness; and all these things shall be added unto you." Matthew 6:33***

Are you seeking the Kingdom of God or the possessions within the Kingdom?

Now let's talk a little about a three-fold relationship with the Godhead. This relationship consists of God the Father, God the Son and God the Holy Ghost/Spirit. They work together and are distinctly separate.

- They are the reason all exists (**Genesis 1**),
- They are the reason we exist (**Genesis 1**),
- We are called by them (**Jeremiah 1:5**).

The reason the "IN" is important is because you can't just have God in your life or just be with God. You have to be in a relationship with the Godhead. Your relationship with God has to get past your flesh(***1 John 2:16***), pass your feelings of hurt (fear, doubt and shame).

When you are in God, you become like the priest of old.

Your relationship takes you into the Holy of Holies with God. You are at THE mercy seat, engaging in a conversation with the Godhead. Your conversations are 2-way. You are talking to God (not asking out of lust or hurt feelings), but you are exalting Him, asking for your day's provision and asking for forgiveness from your sins and on behalf of others. You ask for help for your walk in life so that you are not tempted but delivered. You praise Him for all and declare it with an Amen. I mean, that is what Jesus says in His model prayer to the Disciples (the Lord's Prayer) *(Matthew 6:9-13)*, correct? You then "listen" for the answer that is within the will of God, "IN" your life. The answer will enlist the "IN" word. The "IN" word for this book is **I**mpossible **N**ecessity. To be "IN" God, you must believe that the impossible from man is a necessity with God. (Matthew 19:26)

To the world and people in general, our God is an impossible concept *(Mark 10:27)*. Jesus lets us repeatedly know that with God, all things are possible. The reason that everything is possible with God is because God created everything, and if it was made, it was a *necessity* for the overall will of God.

Can I leave you with this one thing as we go deeper into the different order of the Godhead? In order to be "IN," we first had to be out. At one point, we were not in the family of God. We were out of the saving grace and out of heaven. The blood has placed us "IN" with the Godhead - our body, heart, mind, soul and spirit.

Notes

8

God The Father - Inclusion

The act of including: the state of being included

15 Whosoever shall confess that Jesus is the Son of God, God dwelleth in him, and he in God.

16 And we have known and believed the love that God hath to us. God is love; and he that dwelleth in love dwelleth in God, and God in him. (1 John 4:15-16)

The first person of the Godhead is God, the Father. He goes by many names (actually, the Godhead goes by many names), but for this book and text, God the Father is what we are going to use. The reason I say that is because most of us do not understand the importance of his Fatherhood to us. Some understand it as it refers to Jesus. Some have a thought of God as Father to the entire world, but within a personal relationship where God is a Father to us is a little far-fetched. Yes, He is God, the Maker of the entire world, Creator of everything and yet, He is our Father who deals with our everyday needs.

I can understand why most of us feel that God is not concerned about us or our everyday problems and issues. I felt that way for many years. I saw Him as an angry God looking down on me from heaven, waiting for me to fail so He could condemn me to hell. The sovereign God was not true to me. Most of the sermons I heard as a baby Christian were if you did this or you did that, you were going to hell. At 13 years old, all that guilt and condemnation was a bit much. I could not do anything, but I did learn one thing, go to the altar, pray, and your sins would be forgiven. I did that every

Sunday. I would go to the altar and pray about all the bad things I had done the week before. Cry a little or a lot based on what I did. Go back to the pew and feel better for a day or less. Then go back to being bad because I may have been saved, but I was not delivered from my bad deeds, and I felt the love of God was nowhere near me.

This was not true repentance. This was repetition. I did not feel better for long at all. After a while, I felt nothing. I was just playing a role of a churchgoer. I did not understand what the Father wanted in regard to the desired relationship with me; that I would see him as a caring, loving Father, not as a mean God. Not to see Him as a man but as an eternal Lord that was over all and loves us all. He wanted me to soften my heart towards Him, so I could be included in the family that He wants and desires for me. I had to be "IN" Him to know faith, trust and love towards Him and to enjoy the relationship of inclusion.

Sidebar: Thank you, God, for "real" salvation.

God the Father is the One that includes us. How, you may say? Well, He started it at the beginning. Let's go to *Genesis 1,* where it all began.

Now *Genesis 1* began with them (the Trinity) creating the world and everything that would be needed within it to keep it going. Then in *verse 26,* God says something powerful...

26And God said, Let us make man in our image, after our

likeness: and let them have dominion over the fish of the sea, and over the fowl of the air, and over the cattle, and over all the earth, and over every creeping thing that creepeth upon the earth.

²⁷ So God created man in his own image, in the image of God created he him; male and female created he them.

I hope you see the inclusion God gave to us.
His **image** and after His **likeness**

Image is defined as **a visual representation of something.**

Likeness is defined *as the quality or state of being like:* **RESEMBLANCE**

The image and likeness of God is a heavy mantle to carry, but it brings us into an inclusion like no other creature He has made. We need to be "IN" His image. We must show up as men and women and as a visual representation of God. We must be in the quality or state of being after His likeness.

I want you to think about that. God wants a family that looks like Him. Talks like Him. Loves like Him. And most of all, in love with Him. Adam and Eve started out great! They were walking and talking with God in the Garden. *(Genesis 3:8)* Somehow, they lost their way. They wanted more out of their relationship with God. They went from being "IN" to being "WITH" God. They no longer want to be the image but rather to "be" God. They became flesh before they ate the fruit. "So a man thinks so is he" *(Proverbs 23:7).* God doesn't want a fleshly family but a spirit-filled one. A family that loves Him because He first loved them. God knows we will make mistakes, sin and even deny Him but He does not turn away nor destroys us. He keeps stretching His hand toward us, hoping that we will reach out for His. God wants us to be in Him because we are from Him.

The "IN" started from our creation. The Impossible necessity was "us." We come from a thought. The impossible thought was that we were going to come into being in a hostile world that now fights us daily to destroy us in one way or another. Jesus' birth was not the only birth that was a hard fight. I think about my own birth.

I was born in 1967. My mother had a choice not to have me. I could have been born as a still birth. I was late, and anything could have happened during that time. My life could have ended before I took my first breath. I was a tomboy, so I did some crazy things as a girl and thought nothing of it. I feared little. I was so competitive. One time, I was playing hide and go seek. I almost killed myself. I was in the hall closet hiding, and someone opened the door and scared me but did not find me. I cut my leg on a large glass apple jar in the closet. The only reason they were able to find me was because the blood and apple juice was running up under the door. I still have the scar on the back of my leg to this day. As a teenager, I tried to kill myself 3 times. When God did not let me out of this life, I told Him, "If you are not going to let me die, I'm going to live my life my way. I'm glad He did not listen to this spoiled brat, but He knew that one day I would grow to understand why He needed me to live.

Let me back up just a little bit. God, to most of us, comes off like an absentee Father. When we look back over our lives, a Father is one who is there for us. He is there when you learn to walk and encourages you to come on when you are scared to move. Your father is the one that assists you when you first learn how to ride a bike. He walks into school and lets it be known that nobody better bother you in a bad or negative way. He roots for you as you play basketball or as a contestant in a spelling bee. He is a constant until you push him away, and even so, he is still there. He loves you unconditionally. He never gives up on the love that has bonded the two of you since the moment you were born. That sounds like a great father, right? Did you know that God the Father is actually just like that?

He has been there since the beginning. He has loved you unconditionally (agape is the Hebrew word). He has been there through all of the good, bad, and in-between moments of your life. He is a consistent presence. We church people say he is Omnipresent. For the longest time, I really did not know what that meant. Yes, He is around, but I hadn't felt Him which made it hard to believe. I had moments where His presence felt good, but I had to learn to get out of the flesh and be in the spirit. The church had me believing that the "feelings" was a way of knowing God's presence was around me, but actually, it is a "knowing." It is faith, it's trust, and it's love.

The definition that is in the dictionary works for me. It

states: widely or constantly encountered; common or wide-spread.

I would like to believe that my Father is constantly having an encounter with me. When I wake up, He is there talking to me before I leave for work. He is in the car with me while someone almost runs me off the road, and I say to God, "Get your children!" He widely supports me when I am in His will. His presence has become so familiar that I live for Him. Donnie McClurkin has a song that says," I never knew I would come to know You like this!" It's so true! This rebellious, bratty child of God is so in love with the Father God that nothing else matters but to be "IN" His image and "IN" His likeness as much as I can.

The second inclusion I would like for us to look at is in *Galatians 4:5-7.*

⁴To redeem them that were under the law, that we might receive the adoption of sons.

⁶ And because ye are sons, God hath sent forth the Spirit of his Son into your hearts, crying, Abba, Father.

⁷ Wherefore thou art no more a servant, but a son; and if a son, then an heir of God through Christ.

I know some of you are saying, what about Jesus's birth or His death? Wouldn't that be inclusion? And that answer is yes, but that is a testimony of Jesus, wouldn't you say? I want to talk about ABBA Father.

The Godhead made a decision as a result of the fall in

the Garden (back in Genesis), and we were not included. He would send Jesus to earth to die for us who were excluded. Jesus would redeem us by His blood that would give us the ability to be included not as servants but as sons. Please understand we were once outsiders spiritually, mentally, physically, emotionally, financially and verbally. There were far and in-between moments the spirit of God fell upon the people in the Old Testament. When Jesus redeemed us, we were no longer separated but rather a blessed group of people. He opened up the ability for all mankind that would receive Him to come back unto Him.

God the Father did not include us to just be servants working to please Him but to become sons (a family). We now have a home (heaven) that is ours forever. We have a Father (ABBA Father) that we can go to without any doubt, fear or shame, reservation or hesitation, but rather we can come boldly to the throne of grace and speak to our Father directly. We have an inheritance that is specifically given to us by the Father at the time of our adoption. We will be given on earth and in heaven. We are not without. Everything we could ever need is here within us if only we would accept that we are included in the family by adoption, not foster care. God is not just watching us until our real parents get back. God the Father is not going to give us back to the world. He is not renegotiating our relationship. He has already sealed it. He is our Father, and He loves us so much. We are included in the family of God!

Question: Do we "really" want to be "IN"? Freedom from sin requires a sacrifice, and no, I am not talking about Jesus. I am talking about YOU! What are you willing to sacrifice for the freedom of knowing that without doubts, fear, and shame, the God of everything is a Father to you?

"IN" the Father Questions

What area of you does God the Father not belong "IN"?

How are you going to accept the gift of inclusion?

Do you believe that you are adopted?

Prayer of Inclusion

Dear Father,

I am praying because I would like to say thank you for including me in your family; for thinking of me as a child of yours. You established a plan that made sure I was a part of the family. Thank you for ensuring I will be in heaven with you and be there for all eternity. All You ask is that I have faith, trust and hope in Jesus Christ as Savior and Lord and His love for me. God, please remove all obstacles that would stand in my way of getting to you.

Every day of my life, I am determined to seek You in every way that's been made available through the finished works of Jesus. In the name of Jesus, I pray, Amen.

Notes

9

God the Son Jesus - Position

An act of placing or arranging: such as
a: The laying down of a proposition or thesis
b: An arranging in order

Sweet Jesus, where do we start! First, if you haven't accepted Jesus as your personal Lord and Savior, you are not "IN." If you have not confessed with your mouth and believed in your heart that Jesus's life, death, resurrection, and ascension were for you are not "IN." If you don't believe that Jesus is, right now, seated at the right hand of the Father making intercession for you daily, you are not "IN." If you don't believe He has put away the devil's allegations against you by saying, "Cynthia is covered by the blood!" (I told you to make it personal), you are not "IN."

Side Note: Salvation is the only way into the family of God.

Jesus is the second part of the Godhead. As God the Son, He has given us a position within the family. There are three that I would like to write about.

1. **Position as our Savoir** (John 3:16-18)
2. **Position as heirs** (Galatians 3:28-29)
3. **Position as our Groom** (Matthew 25:1-13)

I will break down each one and why it is important to be "IN."

Position as our Savoir
16For God so loved the world that he gave his only begotten

Son, that whosoever believeth in him should not perish, but have everlasting life

[17]For God sent not his Son into the world to condemn the world; but that the world through him might be saved.

[18]He that believeth on him is not condemned: but he that believeth not is condemned already, because he hath not believed in the name of the only begotten Son of God. (John 3:16-18)

These three scriptures are the roadmap to salvation straight out of Jesus' own mouth. Nicodemus wanted to know how a man could be born again. The discussion is completely fascinating. Jesus is telling an older man that he had to be born again. I think we forget this as we mature in Christ. We have to be born again. It is a daily task that does not leave because you know more scripture, pray better, or in ministries within the church. We have a daily commitment to be grateful and respect the ministry of salvation in our personal lives. It is not over once we say the Sinners prayer. On the contrary, it is just the beginning of your journey. We must be devoted to our Savior. We need to begin to work on doing the will of Jesus. The will of Jesus is not just a rite of passage. His death was not by accident or because the Jews wanted to kill him. He laid down his life so we could have eternal life. Your salvation was the ultimate gift from the Godhead towards you. You would never see eternal life if they had not decided we needed to come back home. We need to be in the family. We need to be "IN." We are no longer outside because Jesus said in *John 14: 6*

"I am the way, the truth, and the life: no man cometh unto the Father, but by me."

The positioning of Jesus has led us to the Father just like His life, death, resurrection, and ascension were supposed to do. As our Savior, His position is to purchase our salvation with His very life. Savior means one that saves from danger or destruction. We were in danger. Sin and death were waiting to take us out into eternal damnation. They are the enemies of holiness and life. That danger was going to place us in hell without a solution. Our Savior came to save us from that danger. It is not enough just to get saved. We must become like Christ. We must become Christians (Christ-like). We can't just be saved for the sake of being saved. We have to live out salvation as a daily lifestyle.

Most of us don't live a life of salvation. We are too busy trying to live a life of prosperity, God and country or some other things that are flesh driven. Salvation is a gift that we should appreciate.

Position as heirs

Galatians 3:28-29
[28] There is neither Jew nor Greek, there is neither bond nor free, there is neither male nor female: for ye are all one in Christ Jesus.

[29] And if ye be Christ's, then are ye Abraham's seed, and heirs according to the promise.

The first thing we must understand is that when God sees us, He sees Jesus Christ, His beloved son. He doesn't see Cynthia but the blood of the lamb. I am "IN" Christ Jesus, and the only person that can take me out of that position is ME.

As heirs, according to the promise, we have been brought into the family of God. We are brought in by the promise made to Abraham and the sacrifice Jesus made on our behalf. You can't have one without the other. The first part is the seed of Abraham. God promised Abraham several times in scripture that he would be the father of many nations. This is one of my favorite scriptures on that:

"Neither shall thy name any more be called Abram, but thy name shall be Abraham; for a father of many nations have I made thee." (Genesis 17:5)

God had a plan for Abraham and his seed. They have become many nations but, unfortunately, divided nations. In Israel, the Israelites and the Palestinians are fighting over land that they believe the other has no claim to possess. The truth is that Ishmael and Isaac made up many years ago, and their descendant's started a war that no one would win without God.

When we start putting conditions on who is the seed, we abort God's promise and Jesus's sacrifice on the cross. We change the promise into a demand and the sacrifice into a pledge. The blessings for the seed of Abraham are obtained by faith. We must believe that God is God. We must believe that Jesus' sacrifice on the cross was to cancel out the debt we could not pay. Trusting in God is how faith works through us. Once we have faith and trust, loving God is not that far behind.

Salvation is not easy but necessary in order to believe the impossible is possible with God. A man dying on a cross for people He did not know seems crazy, but if you have faith, you know that it is true.

You know and understand that this salvation was the ultimate gift from Jesus to us all. He took on the sins of the world not to condemn them but to win them back in total victory. Trusting in the power of the blood rips the veil that once separated us. When we see Jesus as the Savior of our souls and not our flesh, we will work to prosper it and not just our pockets *(3 John1:2)*. The love of Jesus showed up at the beginning and will never leave us nor forsake us. He is a constant Savoir no matter where we are in our kingdom journey.

10

The Bride (The Church) and the Groom (Jesus Christ)

1 Then shall the kingdom of heaven be likened unto ten virgins, which took their lamps, and went forth to meet the bridegroom.

2 And five of them were wise, and five were foolish.

3 They that were foolish took their lamps, and took no oil with them:

4 But the wise took oil in their vessels with their lamps.

5 While the bridegroom tarried, they all slumbered and slept.

6 And at midnight there was a cry made, Behold, the bridegroom cometh; go ye out to meet him.

7 Then all those virgins arose, and trimmed their lamps.

8 And the foolish said unto the wise, Give us of your oil; for our lamps are gone out.

9 But the wise answered, saying, "Not so"; lest there be not enough for us and you: but go ye rather to them that sell, and buy for yourselves.

10 And while they went to buy, the bridegroom came; and they that were ready went in with him to the marriage: and the door was shut.

11 Afterward came also the other virgins, saying, Lord, Lord, open to us.

12 But he answered and said, Verily I say unto you, I know you not.

13 Watch therefore, for ye know neither the day nor the hour wherein the Son of man cometh. Matthew 25:1-13

I tried to find a shorter scripture, but this says it all. Jesus was talking about the church and what we need to be doing while we wait for His return. He worded it in an analogy using a parable about 10 virgins waiting for the bridegroom to come to them.

Now they did not know when He was coming. Would He return in the day or at night, but they had to make sure there was enough oil in their lamps no matter the outcome. As they go about their daily lives (going to work, helping family and friends, shopping and so on), they are waiting.

Out of these 10 virgins, 5 are wise, and 5 are foolish. The wise ones had enough oil for their lamps. They had the Holy Ghost/Spirit inside of them. They were living their lives, but they were always watchful for the voice that would let them know that He was here. In scripture, Jesus says, *"My sheep hear my voice, and I know them, and they follow me..."* **(John 10:27).**

Sidebar: Who are you listening to?

When you are at 90% in God, you are constantly listening for the word of God in your ear. You become tuned in to what He is saying to you. You will begin to walk and talk like Him. You will favor him. The image of God can be seen in you.

When people get married, they do start to look like each other. Their physical appearance stays the same, but their mannerisms become similar. They can finish each other's statements or complete their sentences. They have the same mental and verbal cues. That's what marriage does. It makes a covenant that will bind you together. He has sacrificed His life for your, and He will love you for all eternity. This relationship most people may not understand, but they do respect it. Your love for Him submits to His will and not your own.

Now the foolish virgins were going about their business and were not as watchful about the coming of their groom as the wise virgins. Their business was to get married.

They needed to be aware and prepared for the bridegroom's arrival. They need the oil (the Holy Spirit) the inside of them. They needed His guidance, but they chose not to have it. That sounds a lot like what we should be doing, right? Not complaining that it is taking too long or people have been saying this for centuries. When we are thinking about how and when with God, we are "with" God, but when we wait, we are "IN."

Hearing from God requires us to listen. When we are listening to all the outside noise, our ears can't hear properly. We may have faith, but trusting and loving Jesus is a problem. We get busy trying to be a god to God and changing his will, and before we know it, we are no longer heirs but workers of iniquity (**Luke 13:27**).

I am going to leave you with this scripture. I pray that this is you when it is all said and done:

Let us rejoice and be glad and give the glory to Him, for the marriage of the Lamb has come and His bride has made herself ready." Revelation 19:7

Questions for God Jesus

Who is Jesus to you?

Does He have a place, a home (position) in your life and if so, where?

Can Jesus call on you, and you hear Him?

Prayer To Jesus

"Dear Jesus, thank you for being my Savior and my Lord because, without your sacrifice, I would not be an heir. I want to make sure that I am listening to you, hearing you, and responding because your words give me life. I want to be a bride (the church) that does not rebel but submits to You completely because I know the price that was paid was great. I ask for your forgiveness for every area of my life that I have not given to You. I surrender it all right now in your name, Amen.

Notes____

Notes____

I I

God the Holy Ghost/ Spirit – Location

A position or site occupied or available for occupancy or marked by some distinguishing feature: SITUATION

The Holy Ghost/Spirit is a subject most people are confused about or afraid to understand. The church has not been good when it comes to explaining Him. Yes. I said Him. He is the 3rd person of the Godhead. Jesus introduces Him to the future church in the following scripture in *John 14:26.* **"But the Comforter, which is the Holy Ghost, whom the Father will send in my name, he shall teach you all things, and bring all things to your remembrance, whatsoever I have said unto you."**

Have you ever noticed that you remember things you've heard about as a child? That's the Holy Ghost. Jesus was clear on who He was and what He would be doing. First, the Father would send Him.

Sidebar: Do you see the "location."

Now, he's been sent to us, and He will teach us all things. When we are "IN" the family, we must be taught how to be children of God. We learn how to be His children through the word of God. This is not something that comes to us easily. We are flesh, and our minds have to be transformed to understand the things of the spirit of God. We can't expect to one day accept salvation, and then we are instantly changed. That is reserved for when the rapture comes.

We have work to do in order to be joint heirs with Christ. Now let me stop. I am not talking about works; I'm talking about our souls changing, living in faith, love and trust in

God. I am talking about obedience over sacrifice. Jesus says we MUST worship God in spirit and in truth *(John 4:24)*. We cannot worship God in a fleshly being. He is spirit. We are Spirit, we have a soul, and we live inside these physical bodies. That is why the Holy Ghost is so important. He is located on the inside of each and every one of us who believes in Jesus Christ. He connects us to the Godhead.

The Holy Ghost/Spirit will teach us everything we need to know if we are willing to listen and obey. In the Amplified Bible, it says, **"But the Helper (Comforter, Advocate, Intercessor—Counselor, Strengthener, Standby), the Holy Spirit, whom the Father will send in My name [in My place, to represent Me and act on My behalf], He will teach you all things. And He will help you remember everything that I have told you."** (John 14:26). I love this version because do you see all that the Holy Ghost does for us? He has so many roles in our Kingdom life that we need to take a moment to learn of Him.

Comforter

Jesus says He will be a **Comforter**. Well, what exactly is a Comforter? According to the dictionary, a Comforter is *someone who helps you to feel less worried, upset, frightened, etc.: someone who comforts you.* The Holy Ghost was not sent to scare us but to be a comfort during times of discomfort.

We all go through challenges and difficulties in life. No matter where you are in your walk with God, you will feel worried, get upset and even be frightened, but please know and trust that the Holy Ghost/Spirit is right there to assist. He will comfort you with the words from the Father and Jesus. He will bring back to your remembrance all the other times God brought you through victoriously in the challenges of your life. When the winds were blowing, it seemed like you were going to break in half, but somehow you just stood right back up. The is the Godhead being a fortress and a refuge.

He will help you to see things differently. The Holy Spirit will let you see the end of a thing so you can make it through safely to the other side. He will bring the scriptures to your mind that will bring joy to your heart and soul. He will place a song in your spirit, and the next thing you know, you are dancing and rejoicing in God, remembering all that He has done for you.

Advocate

He is an **Advocate**. An Advocate is *one who pleads the cause of another*. Did you know that people are pleading your case? The Godhead is pleading your cause for salvation and transformation.

The Godhead decided thousands of years ago that you would need salvation. They talked to one another and made it so. The Family wanted no separation and devised a plan that would bring us back home to God. God the Father did his part. Jesus has done his part. Now the Holy Ghost/Spirit is doing His part. He is pleading the case of salvation to the unsaved and the backslider. He is also pleading the cause of transformation to the heirs. He is calling those that are chosen to the Kingdom of God daily, offering the Way into peace, joy and love.

When I first came to God, it didn't happen in a church or revival meeting. Yes, I was as going to church but was but did not understand salvation. I got baptized in water but not in the spirit. A woman gave me a tract at the bus stop, and that was the first time I let God in. The Godhead will come for you and lead you to Themselves. You are not alone with the Family. You are covered.

Intercessor

He is an **Intercessor.** An Intercessor is one who *prays, petitions or entreats in favor of another.* The word of God says that Jesus is an Intercessor for us **(Romans 8:34).** The Holy Ghost intercedes on your behalf as well.

"Likewise the Spirit also helpeth our infirmities: for we know not what we should pray for as we ought: but the Spirit itself maketh intercession for us with groanings which cannot be uttered." We do not always know what to say or what we need to pray for but thank God the Holy Ghost/Spirit speaks on our behalf to God.

He takes the infirmities (*physical or mental weaknesses*) and converts them into prayers. He does this because most of us do not want to admit our weaknesses to Him. Being the God He is, He cannot lie but prays (intercedes) on our behalf so that we would be compelled to admit, repent and be transformed for the glory of God. He takes our inner words and transforms them into the holy language, and sends them to the Father. Jesus and the Holy Ghost/Spirit are interceding on our behalf. All that is required of us is to have faith in God that He will do exactly what He said He would do.

Counselor

He is a **Counselor**. A Counselor is a person who gives advice or recommendations.

Have you noticed that there are times that you feel like you should be doing something? Maybe you feel like you shouldn't be around this particular group of people? Your spirit is uneasy, and you don't know why? That is the Holy Spirit speaking to you.

The Holy Ghost/Spirit speaks to us to advise us on the way to go and what we should and should not do. He, like the rest of the Godhead, is a gentleman. He is not going to "make" you do anything but will give you sound advice on the things that will grow and mature you into your new Family and in the position you have as a child of God.

Strengthener

He is a **Strengthener**. A Strengthener is not in the dictionary, but I have the closest definition. *Strengthen: to make stronger.* Your infirmities, when we are ready to face them, can be used to strengthen our faith. As we grow our faith, trust and love in God (the 90%), we will not keep going out from the Holy of Holies but stay in His presence because we know, without a doubt, God can and will make everything alright.

The Holy Ghost is a strengthener for us. He will give us His word, passages, scriptures and songs to get us through the hard times. Sometimes, it will come out of nowhere, and the next thing we know, we are crying tears of joy because we know the victory is ours. We will start dancing because we are praising God for deliverance in advance. We are rejoicing because we realize that the devil's loss is our gain. He keeps making us stronger through the hurt, pain, trials and tribulations. We need to stop depending on our own mind, body and spirit and give it all to God. We have to cast all of our cares on Him. *(1Peter 5:7).* When we give God our all (spiritually, emotionally, mentally, verbally, financially, sexually and physically) is when we are living in the 90%.

Standby

He is a **Standby**. A Standby is *one to be relied upon, especially in emergencies: a favorite or reliable choice or resource.* I love this definition so much. He is right by Cynthia (make it personal). He is there in the good and bad.

He gives me all the resources I need to live kingdom living right here on earth. I don't have to make this stuff up. I don't have to reinvent the wheel; I just have to go in the direction of the wheel and believe.

When you have someone standing "beside" you, you have someone who is standing "with" you. They will be there to watch your back and make sure you don't get hurt. They will fight for you if it comes to that. They will pray with you so you don't go out of the will of God. They will stand in for you so that you are protected. They will never leave you nor forsake you.

This description is the character and attributes of the Holy Spirit in a nutshell. He doesn't leave us. He is right there from day one when we accepted Jesus as our personal Savior and The Father as the Lord over our lives. We don't have to live alone. He is the Family Member that is here to assist us and help us fulfill our purpose and mission in life.

I am going to leave you with an instruction about your relationship with the Holy Spirit.

"And grieve not the Holy Spirit of God, whereby ye are sealed unto the day of redemption." (Ephesians 4:30)

Questions about the Holy Spirit

Do you have a daily relationship with the Holy Spirit?

Do you love Him or fear Him?

Do you see that you need to get a better understanding of who He is?

Praying About the Holy Spirit

"Dear Father, thank you for sending the Holy Ghost/Spirit to comfort me. I don't know what I would do if He was not here. He is a constant in my heart, mind and spirit. He is teaching me and showing me how to genuinely appreciate Him in all that He does for me. I will try my best not to grieve Him but rather to look to Him for guidance in every area of my life. In Jesus's name, Amen."

Notes

Conclusion

Where are you now? Since you've started reading this book, where are you in your relationship with the Godhead?

Are you having a relationship with God?

Or

Are you "with" God?

Or

Are you "IN" God?

Wherever you are in your growth walk of faith, trust and love are a constant part of your salvation and transformation. You will never be 100% on earth, but you can and should be striving to be at 90%. There should be so much of God in every single one of the pores of your body that you glow like Him. You should desire that people say to you, "You are glowing!" or "There is an air about you that is different!" "You seem peaceful!"

When our faith is like the faith of Abraham (which is the true blessing of Abraham) coinciding with your trust in God, loving Him becomes easy. There is no stopping you from transforming your mind, body and soul away from the world.

You will desire the heavenly things that you can call down into your life.

Jesus, in the scriptures, says,
"Verily I say unto you, Whatsoever ye shall bind on earth shall be bound in heaven: and whatsoever ye shall loose on earth shall be loosed in heaven." *(Mathew 18:18)*

Don't guess or think twice. You are in right standing with God. As the Bible says in *1 Peter* **verses 9-11 it states,**
"But he that lacketh these things is blind, and cannot see afar off, and hath forgotten that he was purged from his old sins.
¹⁰Wherefore the rather, brethren, give diligence to make your calling and election sure: for if ye do these things, ye shall never fall:
¹¹For so an entrance shall be ministered unto you abundantly into the everlasting kingdom of our Lord and Savior Jesus Christ."

You have one thing to know, and that is, YOU are a joint heir. You are "IN"!

Savlation Prayer

SALVATION PRAYER

I do not know Jesus as your personal Savior. I would love it if you would say this prayer:

Dear Father, I come to you today because I realize that I can't make it without you. I have tried everything, and I need you. I confess with my mouth that Jesus came down from heaven and laid down his life for me. He was resurrected on the third day and is now sitting at your right hand. This day I give you me and ask that the Holy Ghost come into my life and guide me from this day on in Jesus's name, Amen.

Welcome to the family; I am so happy for you.

Prayer of the Backslider

Maybe you have known the Lord at one time or another. You haven't really been in a relationship with God recently. I am not judging you. I left the Godhead to follow Islam for 13 years. But I had to come back. If that is you, I have a prayer you can say to come home.

Dear Father, I am sorry that I have let the world take me away from you. I want to come home. I want to have my relationship back with the Godhead. I want to grow to love you again. I want to grow my faith in you again. I need to trust in you so I can become the joint heir you intended me to be. I pray this in Jesus's name Amen.

Cynthia Robinson is a 6-time published Author, Life Coach, Motivational Speaker, and Pastor. She believes that every woman has a purpose and whether that is to be the best mother and wife or a CEO of a Fortune 500 company, they deserve respect in their positions in life.

As an author, she has written several books to empower and inspire the women of God to reach for their best life amid bad circumstances. As a coach, she believes in building up a woman to move forward in their journey and learning to enjoy the process. She is a motivational speaker that ignites the people to go for theirs. Pastor Cynthia is a loving and compassionate soul that knows rebelling against God only brings you to him humble.

She speaks to the hearts of men and women alike through her daily motivational messages on her social media pages and her blog entitled "My Crazy is Real," which is on her website www.CynthiaRobinson.me. She also has a weekly streaming Talk Show called The Crazy Within. She works to change the mindset of women around the world to walk in the royalty they have been called into by God.

Other Books By Cynthia Robinson

- *I Am Leah*
- *You are Cordially Invited*
- *31Reflecyions of a Virtuous Woman Proverbs 31 Devotional Book (eBook only)*
- *The 7 Pillars of a Woman (eBook only)*
- *Know your Crazy, Accept Your Crazy*
- *For Such a Time as This (Collaboration with Paulette Harper)*

References in the Book

Reference within the book are from the King James Version of the Bible unless otherwise stated

Dictionary Reference are from Merriam-Webster